THE SPIRIT OF DISTRICT SIX

THE SPIRIT OF DISTRICT SIX

CLOETE BREYTENBACH

TEXT BY BRIAN BARROW

PURNELL

CAPE TOWN · JOHANNESBURG · LONDON

PUBLISHED BY PURNELL & SONS (S.A.) (PTY.) LTD.,
KEEROM STREET,
CAPE TOWN

SBN 360 00101 7

SET IN 12 PT. ON 14 PT. BASKERVILLE

PRINTED AND BOUND
IN THE REPUBLIC OF SOUTH AFRICA
BY THE RUSTICA PRESS (PTY.) LTD.,
WYNBERG, CAPE.

LITHOGRAPHIC POSITIVES
BY J. ZAMMIT & SON,
CAPE TOWN

CONTENTS

IMPRESSIONS

THE shop-window at the street corner was two feet deep in eggs. There was nothing else in that window, only eggs. And painted on the window in red: 'Mixed Eggs: small, medium, large and extra large. Price 26c a dozen.' Out of the shop came a fearfully old, small, wizened woman, gaping at the world with opaque purple eyes. She could have been looking for some dark corner to lie down and die in. Her face had shrunk to a handful of wrinkles and her toothless mouth was open like an old thirsty tortoise. She gaped and felt her way out of the egg-shop carrying one egg in a black clawed hand. She walked slowly down the pavement, touching passers-by to steady herself, then disappeared into a small butcher's shop bursting with people and raw meat. You couldn't see into the shop through all the meat that hung in the window, pigs' heads, chunks of black liver on marble slabs, whole lambs, cows' ribs, ox tails, haunches of beef, bowls of mince and curtains of sausages. Everyone in the shop gave way spontaneously to let the old woman reach the counter. There was always a deep respect for the very old in District Six, even fear, for the old were so much wiser and nearer death. A black hand came through the thick curtain of sausages and five dirty fingers dug into the bowl of mince and pulled out a fistful of it, a well-judged pound for the old woman. She emerged from the shop with her egg in one claw and her mince in the other. Now she was more uncertain, she had no free hand with which to steady herself; but a young Moslem in a red fez appeared, put his arm round her frail old back and helped her on her way.

It was District Six on a Saturday morning, on many Saturday mornings, on every Saturday morning that I have been there. Hanover Street: a river of people, cars, barrows, buses, horse-drawn carts and small boys racing down slopes in soap box carts; a bustling, laughing, hooting, whistling, shouting, chatting river of people; fat women with scarves round their heads laden with shopping-bags, a turbaned sheik in long robes and a neat hair-line moustache, pretty young Coloured girls with large gaps in their teeth; men looking like King Farouk with smart suits, dark glasses and tarbooshes; two little girls with coloured chalks, drawing pictures on the pavement; an old Moslem, blind in one eye, selling green ginger, garlic and chillies; young men with skin-head haircuts and brass-studded belts ogling girls at street corners and girls swinging sexy backsides; men hurrying by with blocks of ice on their backs, or large bags of sweet potatoes or sacks with gallon jars of white wine; messengers, fah-fee runners, cripples, skollies, loafers, dope-peddlars, men and women with haunting faces—oriental, Arabic, Semitic, European, Hottentot, African, people whose faces were the faces of Malaya, India, Ceylon, Mauritius, Mozambique, Africa, Western and Eastern Europe, all blending with one another but each somehow retaining a shadow of its origins.

Hawkers set up their barrows at nearly every street corner with pyramids of nartjies, oranges and apples, bunches of bananas, green mounds of avocado pears and trays of wild figs. 'Fresh apples master, six for a bob.' Tomatoes, onions, carrots, radishes, potatoes, beetroot, cucumbers, squash. Peels, paper and plastic bags in all the gutters. At the fish market, red roman, fresh snoek, silver fish and geelbek gleaming on cold stone slabs. Children everywhere. Shouting, laughing, whistling, teasing, darting between old men's legs, running between fast-moving buses and cars and missing them by inches with perfect judgement; children who all seemed too thin, too small, too old and wise for their ages, playing in dirty gutters, dark alleys and sitting in dark doorways with stairs leading straight up from the pavement to mysterious rooms. But children who were always laughing, playing with anything they could find and putting it to good use: discarded boxes, tins, old car-tyres, pram wheels, hoops of iron, ball-bearings, children playing hopscotch in the middle of busy streets, singing, skipping or kicking footballs made of rolled-up newspapers. Poor, underfed children, but cheeky, confident, happy and so emotionally secure in the bosom of their sordid surroundings. Everyone loved them. To them, it seemed, every adult in those busy streets was another mother, another father.

The variety and number of shops was always bewildering. At one time there were more barber-shops to the square acre than anywhere else in the world: 'The Ethiopian Hairdressers', 'The Grand Canyon Barber Shop', 'The Gay Life', 'Personality Plus' and names like that. Tailors, butchers, fruiterers, fishmongers, milliners, spice and curry shops, shoe-shops, hardware and porcelain shops and general dealers, everything. There was the general dealer who had so much in his shop and such a variety of goods that only one customer at a time could get into it. Banjoes, guitars, mandolins, prams and chairs hung from the ceiling. The shop-window was packed with hundreds of different items all price-tagged as extra-special bargains. At a glance you saw glass vases, cups, kettles, lamps, razors, a scale, oil-stoves, kitchen utensils, broom-heads, fly-sprays, chamber-pots, mops, batteries, a scale, pots, pans, cheese-graters, jars, kettles, torches, locks, clocks, clothes-pegs, thermos flasks, rolling-pins, egg-beaters, knives, rope, porcelain ornaments of dogs, cats, birds, reindeer and squirrels, ash-trays, rolls of linoleum in red floral patterns, belts, Jew's-harps and mouth-organs. The little Jewish shop-owner told us his philosophy, his secret for success: 'If you've got it, someone will buy it.'

Then there were those small dimly-lit little shops that sold herbs and spices and aromatic joss-sticks or '*meangstokkies*' which Moslems burnt in their homes on certain nights to keep away evil spirits. In one of them served an old dignified man with a white turban and a silver beard. He and his son also made round plaques with Arabic inscriptions from the Koran, all done in iridescent gold, green, red, blue and purple. They were called 'Rakaams' and all good Moslems hung them on their walls like icons.

*　　*　　*

In District Six the meanest coin always meant something, a penny or a cent or even a half cent had worth. You could buy one cigarette if you wanted it, one cigarette for a cent and men like Babs Essop who was always kind to the very poor, whose shop was at the corner of Lavender Hill, would even sell half a cigarette for half a cent. The people were very poor round there. They lived for the day, for the moment. They never bought two eggs if one would do. Little urchins arrived with coins clutched in their hands as if they were diamonds. They were always doing shopping errands for their mothers and they would ask for an 'oulap patiselle' (a penny's worth of parsley), a 'tikkie swart bekkies' (black-eyed beans), a 'sixpence soup-greens', a 'tikkie knofelok' (garlic), an 'oulap rissies' (chillis) or an 'oulap broos' (a penny's worth of bruised fruit).

Down the hill along Hanover Street was one of the most charming of the many spice shops, five feet wide, seven feet long and behind the small counter in the dusky interior a beautiful Moslem girl with an embroidered silk shawl over her shoulders, weighing little packets of curry powder in an old scale. She had been mixing spices in beautiful large ornate bowls made of Malayan silver which had been in her family for many generations. One of her ancestors had brought them from the East. He was a nobleman and his wife brought many secret curry recipes which they sell to this day. This girl behind the counter had delicate ivory hands and her face had the frail transparent quality of a china teacup. It was a face any man would wish to hold in his hands. She worked and lived with spices and she seemed very much a part of the rich aromatic atmosphere of her surroundings. There were shelves laden with beautiful jars of spices: fine cinnamon, cloves, fine nutmeg, whole aniseed, cayenne pepper, angelica (the name reminded one of her), mustard seed, thyme, cardamom, fennel; and so many spices with Indian names like methie, jiera, badia, koljanna,

3

masala and sajiera.

Her father had gone to the Muir Street Mosque to pray; five times a day he and all other good Moslems prayed, before sunrise, at midday, in the afternoon, at sunset and after sunset and they said beautiful simple prayers which were a form of grace, thanking Allah for the senses of touch, smell, taste, sight, hearing. How devout and dignified these people were and how much their religion meant to them, and with what sincerity they lived it in their daily lives. In the spacious, tapestried silence of the Muir Street Mosque were these words:

> Enthusiasm is the vehicle of my life
> Contemplation of Allah is my compassion
> Faith is the source of my power
> Sorrow is my friend
> Knowledge is my weapon
> Truth is my salvation
> Worship is my habit
> Love of all men is the core of my belief.

* * *

Another Saturday morning in District Six where anything could happen and everyone in the end would laugh about it. Everything there seemed to end in laughter, even tragedy. There was that Saturday morning when a magistrate at Caledon Square had to enforce a suspended sentence on a skollie found guilty of 'assault with intent to do grievous bodily harm', a suspended sentence of six months' hard labour, and the magistrate passed this sentence with great sombreness and gravity, so that tough old skollie in the dock felt sorry for him. He was a skollie all right with his round hat pressing down on his ears. His face broke into a big smile. 'Nevermind, Boss', he said to the magistrate as they led him down to the cells, 'no hard feelings'. The courtroom erupted with laughter. The court orderly jumped to his feet. 'Silence! Silence!'

Yes, it was a place where anything could happen. There was that Saturday morning when all the traffic in Hanover Street was held up by a game of football. Someone produced a ball and everyone started kicking it. There was uproar. Cars and buses hooted angrily, but it all ended in laughter when the ball bounced resoundingly on to the roof of a beautiful new midnight-blue Mercedes. To cap it all a moffie appeared on the scene. Young men gave him wolf whistles and small boys threw orange peels at him. Near by in Cannon Street a mentally-retarded youth stood in the doorway of his home with an expression of anguished concentration, listening to a ping-pong ball which he held between his thumb and forefinger close to his ear. On the opposite pavement walked two small Malay boys wearing spats, immaculately-cut tailor-made suits and white knitted skull-caps. And then the ultimate case of the blind leading the blind: a

4

drunk blind man being led through the crowds by a man who was blind drunk. People turned, gave way and roared with laughter at their disastrous progress.

*   *   *

Then those sudden moments of spontaneous mischief or gaiety, or both: the time when a lorry carrying four beautiful white tailor's dummies stopped in Canterbury Street, naked dummies with perfectly formed thighs and breasts. Four skollies who had just shared a bottle saw their chance, or were they prompted by that irrepressible sense of humour? And did the policeman who saw them think of arresting the skollies and the dummies under the Immorality Act? Because within seconds each of them had a beautiful white dummy in his arms and did a little dance or *jol* right there in the street. Everyone laughed, even the policeman.

District Six and the Coons. They belonged together. The Coons in their flaming silks of white, red, yellow, orange, green, blue, their dancing and prancing, their vivacity, their unquenchable happiness and good humour: they were the spirit of District Six come to vibrant, thrilling life. They turned the streets into rivers of fire. They were madness gone sane, they were fantasy turned into reality, they were a heart-throb that gave life to an otherwise dead city. They lived, they danced, they laughed, they drank, they created happiness and infected everyone else with it. The Coons; they really gave something.

*   *   *

District Six on a Saturday morning in the rain, when little boys would take it for granted that they could walk with you under the shelter of your umbrella and when at the end of the block they would demand a few cents for giving you that privilege. When the streets were more deserted than usual and you became more aware of the homes, the buildings and all the slogans painted on the walls. 'You are now in fairyland.' The fairyland where love, happiness, kindness, tolerance and squalor existed side by side. Not far away was that narrow untidy street rotting in the dampness. The pavements and gutters held the accumulated muck of many years. The street-cleaners never bothered to go up there.

Old clothing stuck in the mud, discarded boots, old tins, broken bottles, bones, feathers and pieces of broken glass were the playthings of small Coloured children who laughed and cried incessantly and filled the street with noise and movement. The old peeling houses were in various stages of dilapidation, huddled together as if seeking some communal consolation, and everywhere was the heavy prevalent smell of sour drains, wet fowl-runs, cats, dogs, rats and over-flowing refuse-bins.

Drury Lane, Clyde Street, Kent Street, Arundel Street, Rotten Row, Vernon Terrace and Canterbury Street. The clouds parted and the sun came out like

5

a sword illuminating their hopeless, tired charm, even beauty; little rows of houses with names like 'Wy Wurry' creeping up the slopes of Devil's Peak in colours of white, yellow, green, blue, pink, brown, turquoise, orange, blue and unashamed red. And the warehouses and flats with messages of love, faith, hope and condemnation scratched or painted on the walls. 'Jesus heals, saves and satisfies.' 'The Kingdom of God is at Hand. Repent ye and believe the Gospel.' 'Johannie Titus loves Maisie Mercurio.' *'Piet Pompies is 'n Poep.'* On the walls of a block of flats: 'Stalag 17'. Below that: 'Give me a sailor any day.' 'I'm one. Are you one too?'

The crazy architecture that had somehow just grown with the people. Cross Street, the double cul-de-sac with one end colliding with the wall of the Star Cinema and the other running into the entrance of the City Mission Hall. Butler Square, the size of an average sitting-room, the smallest square in the world. Look down on District Six from some vantage point and the impression it gives is one of unity in diversity, a confused and disorganized abstraction of rusted roofs, turrets, minarets, towers, arches, ornate façades, colonnades and Gothic spires, dazzling in their variety and colour.

*   *   *

But District Six would be nothing without its people and their way of life. Above all it was one of the world's great meeting-places of people of many races, religions and colours and it proved that none of these things really matters. It had a fundamental honesty in that no man or woman who lived there tried to be anything but what he was. And this perhaps was the real secret of the happiness of District Six. There was no bluff and everyone knew where he stood, knew what was attainable and what was not. At times it was a place of violence. But mostly it was a place of love, tolerance and kindness, a place of poverty and often degradation, but a place where people had the intelligence to take what life gave them and give it meaning.

PEOPLE

The Polony Maker

ACHMAT ALLIE the blockman sat behind the marble counter of the Moslem Butchery off Hanover Street. He seemed to be hiding himself behind the high brass scale and the cash register machine, and he was in a sweat of pain and concentration. He had forgotten about the customers because at that moment there weren't any, he had forgotten about all the meat hanging on those large steel hooks, he paid no attention to two cows' heads that lay bleeding on a wooden table near by, he shook his head impatiently when a messenger boy tried to help him. When he saw me he said in Afrikaans, 'Just wait a bit', then he went back to his task, concentrating all the mental and physical resources of his old shrunken body on extracting one of his own teeth.

He had only two teeth left. The one he was tugging at was in front at the bottom, yellow with age. He was loosening it with a pair of pliers and a piece of cloth, his eyes tightly closed. When the tooth was loose he called for some string which the boy gave him. He tied one end round the tooth and the other to the handle of the door. 'Nou', he grunted and the boy slammed the door. The tooth flew out with flecks of blood. Achmat Allie sucked on the hole with his tongue, lips and hollow cheeks, then he stuffed some salt into it with a cracked forefinger and looked up at me, as if to say, 'Well, it's all over now'.

'I've never been to a dentist in all my life', he explained in a shrill cracked voice. 'I don't trust those people. I've pulled out all my own teeth myself, just like you've seen now, just a *tang* and a piece of string and out it comes. Now I've only got one tooth left.'

It was a bottom eye-tooth, stained yellow and brown, the biggest tooth I'd ever seen in the head of a man, and it looked even bigger in the small head of this particular man, about half an inch wide at the gum and about half an inch high, like a fang.

All thought of buying some of his sausages had vanished. Achmat Allie put on a pair of blue-tinted glasses with thin silver rims. He must have worn them out of habit because they settled on the end of his nose and his dry faded old eyes never looked through the lenses. He wore a red fez and a long khaki dust-coat which covered his feet and trailed in the sawdust on the floor.

If I didn't want to buy any sausages, that was that; so he went on with his work, happily answering my questions. His work was to cut dogs' meat out of the two cows' heads. He took up a long knife in fingers that looked like black roots and expertly cut off every bit of meat which gave off a stench that went straight to the pit of the stomach. Soon only the white bovine skulls and huge jawbones were left and the eyes still in their sockets looking remarkably alive and full of cow-like expression. Dead as they were, they seemed to have thoughts behind them. They seemed more alive than Achmat Allie's eyes, which were small and dry and staring.

'Yes, it's for dogs' meat', he said, cutting away with blood-soaked hands, and suddenly he seemed to get a bit testy as if his real status in life had been publicly lowered. 'But this is not my real job, you know. My real job is a polony maker.' He looked up to make sure that this important fact had struck home.

Then he spoke about his life, the house where he was born in District Six, how he went to France in the First World War, his two wives who had died, his children and grandchildren, how he made his own special kind of polony mixed with herbs and spices, the hundreds of sheep's throats he had cut with that same knife, Moslem style; and how, as Allah would witness, he had always tried to kill swiftly and painlessly. And now he was 80 and when he looked back on his life everyone and everything seemed so far away.

And what about his future? Was there anything left for him to do after having lived so much?

'I don't mind telling you a secret', he said in all seriousness. 'Yes, I don't mind telling you. I wouldn't mind getting married again. But she'd have to be young and pretty.

The Man in Saffron

A NUMBER of Indians gathered in a small house on the fringes of District Six to observe the Night of *Divali*, which is always celebrated with the Festival of *Luxmi*, the Hindu Goddess of Light. That year the feast fell towards the end of October. It was a special occasion for local Hindus because the Swami Venkatesananda had come all the way from his monastery at Rishikesh in the Himalayas to bring them a message of spiritual renewal.

It was dark when the holy man arrived. Scores of little clay lamps burnt on the dwarf wall of the veranda, on the gate-posts in front of the house and along both sides of the path leading to the front door. The main room had been turned into a shrine. The walls were garlanded with flowers and more flowers and lamps were set out round a small statue of *Luxmi*, the Goddess of Light. The man in the saffron robes came out of the darkness into the flickering lamplight with the mesmeric eyes of a snake, which were given a strange intensity by the small red dot tattooed between his brows. But it was more a spiritual intensity than an emotional one, few men could have been more self-controlled. The short-cut grey hair, the gentle manner, his calm unlined face with its silent reserves of strength signified a yogic discipline of body and mind. But there was also a sense of humour, wisdom and tolerance, a deeply religious man who through years of study, meditation and self-denial had become the personification of everything he preached. He had travelled all that way from the Himalayas without money, food or personal possessions. In fact he owned nothing except his saffron robes, a rosary of glass beads, a pair of *padukas* (wooden sandals), his own religious writings and the *Bhagavad Gita*, a scriptural work declaring the Hindu belief in the peace and brotherhood of all mankind.

He lived on the charity of his followers, no possessions, absolute renunciation not only of material and physical things but of his own individuality, which

9

The 'Jet Set Hairdressing Saloon'

CHARLIE did not look like a gent's hairdresser and his shop did not look like a 'jet set hairdressing saloon'. Charlie looked like this: His face was dark and much too big for his wide-set beady eyes which were potentially friendly and suspicious. He had five days' growth of grey and black stubble on his jowly cheeks, hair grew aggressively out of his ears and his nostrils, he had a black oily polo-neck jersey which did not smell of after-shave lotion. Beneath it were the contours of a well-developed chest and a fine amiable paunch, beneath which was a pair of sagging trousers held up by a Boy Scout belt with 'Be prepared' on the round buckle. His hands were not exactly the hands of a gent's hairdresser. They were big with thick strong fingers and black dirty fingernails.

His hairdressing saloon looked like this: The entrance was on the corner of one of those narrow roads that lead off Constitution Street. The windows had been boarded up with boxwood, but light came from two cold cathode tubes suspended from the ceiling with flex and looking very much like the bars a trapeze artist uses in a circus. They flickered off and on.

There was something beautiful in the total chaos of the place. Against one wall was a garden bench on which the customers waited. Just then there weren't any customers. The wall on the left of the bench was piled up with used car-tyres, a car-engine, a lawn-mower, tins of paraffin, a step-ladder which was obviously used to reach a high shelf stacked with big plastic containers of liquid brilliantine. There were also pots of engine grease, an old Imperial typewriter and a number of carpenter's tools.

Piled against the opposite wall were some old picture-frames, pieces of timber, a sewing-machine, two wicker basket chairs, coils of rope and stacks of old sacks and newspapers.

There were two barber's chairs, old cowboy-type chairs made in St. Louis, Alabama, in 1906. They were the swivelling tripod type of chair, each with three brass feet, green leather arm-rests and ornately carved wooden back-rests. The confusion really became confusing when you looked at Charlie's hairdressing table, stacked full of hair-oil bottles, soap, cut-throat razors, shaving-brushes, scissors, cracked hand mirrors, cash-books, ash-trays, accounts, invoices and comics. There was also a large oil-can which marine engineers used to lubricate the engines of ships but which Charlie used for dispensing his red liquid brilliantine. The mirrors were both taken from old-fashioned dressing-tables and were hung from the ceiling in the carved wooden frames.

Most of the tiles on the wooden floor were worn through and the floor itself was saturated with oil. Nevertheless Charlie had a man on the job scrubbing the floor and the tiles with soap and water. 'You've got to keep up a certain standard,' he said, 'otherwise the health people get on to you.'

That was fair enough. But why the rest of the junk? Why the organized chaos? Why a hairdresser's saloon called the JET SET that looked like something between a garage and a swop shop?

'I'll tell you why', said Charlie, who still looked friendly and suspicious. 'My father taught me this trade forty years ago. I've been in District Six for 56 years. I taught the trade to my two sons and I've set them up in business. Things went well, but times have changed, as you know. People are moving out. The place is dying. All the bars have closed down. The shebeens have started up again. One place sells a thousand gallons of wine a week. The skollie gangs have started again. In the old days it was the Iron Gang, the Red Cat Gang, the Globe Gang. Now it's the Hungry Hills, the Dirty Dozen and the Bun Boys. Look at my windows, all boarded up. Why? Because every night someone broke in and went off with the till. I got tired of putting in new windows. In the days when this saloon looked posh I had to pay them protection money to make sure they would leave me alone.

'Today I'm a wiser man. Today I can leave my shop with the doors wide open and cash in the till and no one will even dream of entering the place. Why? Because dilapidation means protection.

'Yes, my friend', he said with narrow-eyed conviction. 'It's not all that posh and beautiful. It doesn't smell of men's perfume or after-shave lotion. But that is no standard to judge by.

'I know I'm still the best barber in this town.'

The Tattoo Artist

THE tattoo artist still had his shop in Upper Darling Street about five years ago. He was a man in his mid-thirties with a sallow, lean face and a thick patch of black hair. The arch of his nostrils was somehow made to look more arch by the neatly trimmed hairline moustache on his upper lip. He had dreamy eyes with heavy lids and he wore a white cloak stained with dyes above the breast pocket which made him look like a doctor. When you knocked at the door of his shop, you had to wait a few minutes before it was opened by a young apprentice in his teens who wouldn't let you in unless you had an appointment or stated your business. After telling you to wait the door would be closed and locked while a quick consultation went on inside. Finally, if you 'passed' you would be let into the reception room. The reason for all the secrecy was at that stage obscure. There was never any law against tattooing human bodies. But perhaps tattoo artists were rather odd; in a strange way they were often associated with Black Magic. They had powers. The marks they made on your skin had a certain significance, they could cast a spell over you for life, they could protect you from any harm, they could bring you love and happiness and wealth. This is what many people thought in District Six. A man didn't have his skin punctured, with all the discomfort involved, for nothing. There were mysterious, unknown powers, strange meanings which only the tattoo artist himself could tell you about.

His rooms were rather shabby. There were faded black velvet curtains in the reception room and on a high wooden stand in the corner a stuffed crow. There was a round table and chairs. You could have had quite a good séance in that room. It was cut off by a thin green wall of hardboard with a red curtain for a door and beyond this thin wall was the 'surgery', which smelt of dyes and turpentine.

You could peep through the curtain. The tattooist was busy tattooing something on the smooth bald pate of a middle-aged man with a paunch. He sat in a barber's chair. The tattoo on his bald head was a large butterfly with wings of red and blue. It was something very private, very delicate. Every man has his motives, but you can't very well ask him why he should want a red and blue butterfly tattooed on his bald head.

He left the 'surgery' with his hat on. It was now for the tattooist himself to tell all these secrets. His 'surgery' was full of needles, pairs of scissors, little porcelain bowls and bottles of dye—some he had made himself, some came from South America where the Indians had been using them for centuries. Their ingredients were a secret. The tattooist had long, thin, effeminate hands and a lot of dye under his fingernails. He was inscrutable and uncommunicative at first, then agreed to talk about his craft only if his name was never mentioned.

'You see, my professional honour is at stake', he said somewhat pretentiously. 'Naturally a tattooist wants to make money, but he also has certain standards of decency. Most of my customers are decent people. If a man wants the Rock of Ages tattooed on his backside, I will do it. That is reasonable. But what some people want tattooed on their bodies will shock you. They will pay any price for it too, especially women and they are nearly always well-to-do White women. The things they want tattooed on their stomachs and thighs will shock you. The tattoos some of them have asked me to do would be a blot on my honour. I'm a good church man, you see, a Methodist.'

With the moral issues of tattooing dispensed with he eventually told the absorbing story of the tattooist's art and his place or rather his role in a complex society like District Six where gangs, clubs, class distinctions and superstitions abounded.

It seemed that the urge to have various parts of one's body covered with signs, symbols and ornamentation was an atavistic primitive one that still survived among rich and poor in the most advanced and civilized societies. The reasons why the primitive people of America, Africa and South East Asia tattooed their bodies still applied: superstition, sexual attraction, religious belief or the desire to display symbols of courage, love, mourning, good luck, good health or fraternity. In District Six most habitual criminals had five dots, like the dots on dice, tattooed on their arms or hands. Four of the dots represented the four walls of a prison cell and the fifth dot in the middle was the man imprisoned by the four walls. Many dope peddlars and addicts had three dots tattooed on their hands or arms or foreheads, and prostitutes, homosexuals and lesbians had other identifying signs. In District Six there were many tattoo fetishists. Crosses were guardian angels. During the war many young men had 'Death before Dishonour' tattooed on their chests or forearms. Scores of people had tattoos of mourning, crosses, angels and tombstones. One eccentric had a collar and tie tattooed round his neck; another had 'opened by mistake' tattooed across an appendix scar. A man who had a naked girl tattooed on his stomach had to have a garment tattooed over her nakedness before he could get married. Many young lovers had the shape of their girl friends' lips tattooed on their arms and thighs. A beggar had 'Please' tattooed in the palm of his left hand and 'Thank you' tattooed in the palm of his right. Generally women fetishists liked snakes, dragons and all kinds of phallic symbols tattooed on various parts of their bodies; men liked roosters, eagles, swords, lions and ships.

'I cannot tell you more', the tattooist said. 'I have my professional reputation to think of.'

The Guardian

THE last time I used the public lavatory at the bottom of Upper Darling Street the man in charge was Abubaker Jaffa. He was a dark man, big, strong and level-headed; intelligent, too, with a sharp sense of humour. He made everyone feel welcome. He was not the sort of man to let his job get him down because he had many other interests; in any case it pleased him to be able to perform such a necessary public service. He somehow set the whole atmosphere of the place, which was one of cheerfulness and optimism, and he kept it very clean. The porcelain was spotless and the old brass plumbing shone brightly. The public notices were well displayed. One gave advice on venereal disease, the other two were 'Spitting Prohibited, Penalty £5' and 'Stand close in'. Even from the street it looked like a place with some character. It was quaintly situated in a small park with a profusion of trees and shrubs and good show of flowers in the spring: petunias, daisies, zinnias and marigolds. Not many municipalities are so aesthetically-minded about their public lavatories.

It was Abubaker's job to keep order, see that no one got up to any kind of mischief, make sure that everything functioned smoothly, collect the small fee of a cent per man and hand out the toilet-rolls. He did this automatically while he talked about his real interest in life, the ritual of what is commonly known as a *khalifa*. The performance was really called a *ratieb*, he said: *he* was actually the Khalifa or the man in charge of the *ratieb*. But he had taken part in many performances himself; his arms bore many sword scars, so did his stomach. He had stuck skewers through his cheeks and tongue and the scars were there to show it.

Whatever the spectators thought about a *ratieb* (many people believe it is faked) it was something Abubaker Jaffa took very seriously, regarding it as a test of his faith in the power of the mind over matter. He described the burning of incense, the songs intoned in Arabic, the beating of tambourines and the final state of ecstasy when the mysterious sword dance was performed. Swords would be slashed against forearms and drawn across stomachs, skewers would pierce ear-lobes, tongues and cheeks. The flesh was pierced and cut but there would be no blood. It has mystified medical men for centuries.

The public lavatory, euphemistically called a chalet, of which Abubaker was the official guardian suddenly became quite full with black men, brown men and white men all standing close in and shoulder to shoulder. It was this multi-racialism that made it such a special part of District Six. There were other multiracial toilets in the city but none of them with quite the same character as this one.

'Here there is racial peace and harmony', he said rather proudly. 'No one can do anything about it. The law is too complicated so the Government just leaves us alone.'

He said he had read about the laws somewhere and if the Government wanted to bring apartheid to his lavatory they would have to pass a special Act of Parliament signed by the State President. He was no fool when it came to the law and the law as it stood could only be applied to a public place. His toilet was not exactly a public place because everything that people did in it was done in private. No one who came in there actually occupied the place and the law said that occupation was necessary if they were going to bring in apartheid. When it came to cafés and bioscopes the law said you occupied the place if you sat down, but in his toilet most of the customers stood up and those who sat down did so because of an act of God.

'No, it can never happen here', he said. 'Besides, everyone here is happy. And besides it would take a special Act of Parliament signed by the State President.'

The Fiddler

MANY people will remember him, for you simply could not walk past him and ignore him without it being on your conscience. If you didn't toss a coin in his hat you would walk off worrying about it, thinking that some terrible vengeance lay in store for you. Mothers used to give their small children a cent to drop in his hat as a first lesson in human charity. Even tramps who were hard up themselves used to give him something.

He was always there early in the morning and last thing at night long after everyone had left work and gone home. He stood there all day at the bottom of Queen Victoria Street near the Anglican Church bookshop. He was a small thin emaciated man with large moist eyes that looked like lights in his head. He had sunken cheeks and an Adam's apple made large by a thin stalk of a throat. His trousers ended above his bare ankles and his shoes were too big for his small naked feet. The sleeves of his jacket were too short, showing thin, brittle, transparent arms like those of an opium smoker. He must have had a beggar's licence because the police never picked him up and his way of begging was to place his oily-rimmed hat on the ground to one side of him. When no one was approaching he would stand leaning against the fence as if fast asleep and his chest would rise and fall with an effort. But as soon as someone came along, he would take up his violin with its one string, cup it under his chin with a dirty silk handkerchief, put his bow to the string and saw off a little tune. He probably didn't know a note of music and in all likelihood he couldn't even play the violin, but he went through the motions of playing and the little whine that came wafting towards you on the south-east breeze was tuneful enough to bring back a memory or touch your sympathy. Often passers-by would remark 'How pathetic!' 'The poor little devil, I must give him something', or words to that effect.

That was the little fiddler. Where he went after it was dark and where he came from early every morning to start another day no one ever knew. He was in fact something of a mystery.

Now the thread of this story must shift to District Six where, in those days, Charlie Terblanche with his beautiful rolling Swartland *brei* ran the old Cheltenham Hotel. As soon as Charlie took over the Cheltenham it became the meeting-place of all the characters, especially after five in the evening when they all pitched in for a drink, mostly for any number of drinks; and the strange thing about this situation was that Charlie Terblanche was an ex-detective and they all came to drink at Baas Charlie's bar because many of them were ex-criminals who had had professional dealings with Charlie when he was on the beat. Yes, many of the men he had once arrested for murder, assault, robbery, housebreaking and theft were now his devoted customers and they respected him as they would someone very special. And he loved them, too. 'What characters, man', he would say in his rolling Malmesbury *brei* and he would point to one and then the other. 'They're just liquorice all-sorts', Charlie used to say and by that he meant that in the Cheltenham bar you could meet up with hoodlums, drunks, dope peddlars, pick-pockets, beggars, queers, bores, chancers and no-hopers. Some drank in confidential huddles, some drank alone, fixing their eyes on one spot, some were argumentative and some were happy and full of bawdy laughter, some drank with a strange solemnity.

'Do you see that man there?' said Charlie Terblanche, 'I once arrested him for murder. He got ten years and now he's out again and on the strait and narrow.'

Then he pointed to a tall man who drank his double brandies with a strange ritual. He was always alone and would never take a drink unless he could stand at his own special place in the bar, against the far wall. That was where he was now. He was a tall, sullen man who had a face of disturbed memories. He spoke to no one and looked fixedly before him. Each time before he raised his glass he first looked to the left and then to the right; then he would bring the glass slowly to his mouth, allow his eyes to roll round the rim and empty the contents with a single, convulsive swallow.

'That man', said Charlie, 'was one of the greatest safe-breakers in the business. The safe wasn't made that he couldn't open. Except one. And that was a famous case, I can tell you. He and two others broke into a place in Long Street. But the safe weighed 800 pounds and they couldn't get it open. They took it away with them mind you! Just the three of them. And you know how?' And here Charlie Terblanche's Malmesbury *brei* added to his powers of description:

'They rolled it out of the shop on billiard balls.'

A year passed before my next visit to Charlie Terblanche and the Cheltenham and this time he was more excited about his characters than ever. 'Now,' he said, 'I want to show you the greatest character of them all. That bloke sitting over there.'

It was the little fiddler. But he now looked a very sick man. His large eyes were brighter and wetter than ever, his neck and arms thinner, his breathing more laboured, with upward jerks of his chest. He sat at a table with his hat on, his violin on his left and in front of him a tumbler of Scotch whisky.

'He looks poor, but he makes more money in a day than the rest of them put together', said Charlie. 'After every day's begging he takes a taxi from the bottom of Queen Victoria Street to here, and he sits at that table till the bar closes and drinks nothing but the best Scotch. Sometimes he buys drinks for everyone in the bar. Once he told me if I was short of cash he'd let me have some. But death is staring him in the face, I can tell you. He's riddled with TB. They told him at Groote Schuur that if he didn't lay off liquor he would die. But he told the doctors they knew nothing about life and that he would live it his own way. Now there's a character for you.'

Charlie Terblanche shouted to him across the noise of the bar. The fiddler took a deep painful breath and looked up. It seemed then that death really was staring him in the face and that he was staring back.

But when he saw Charlie he raised his glass and smiled, a wonderful toothless smile that pinned back his ears with its radiance.

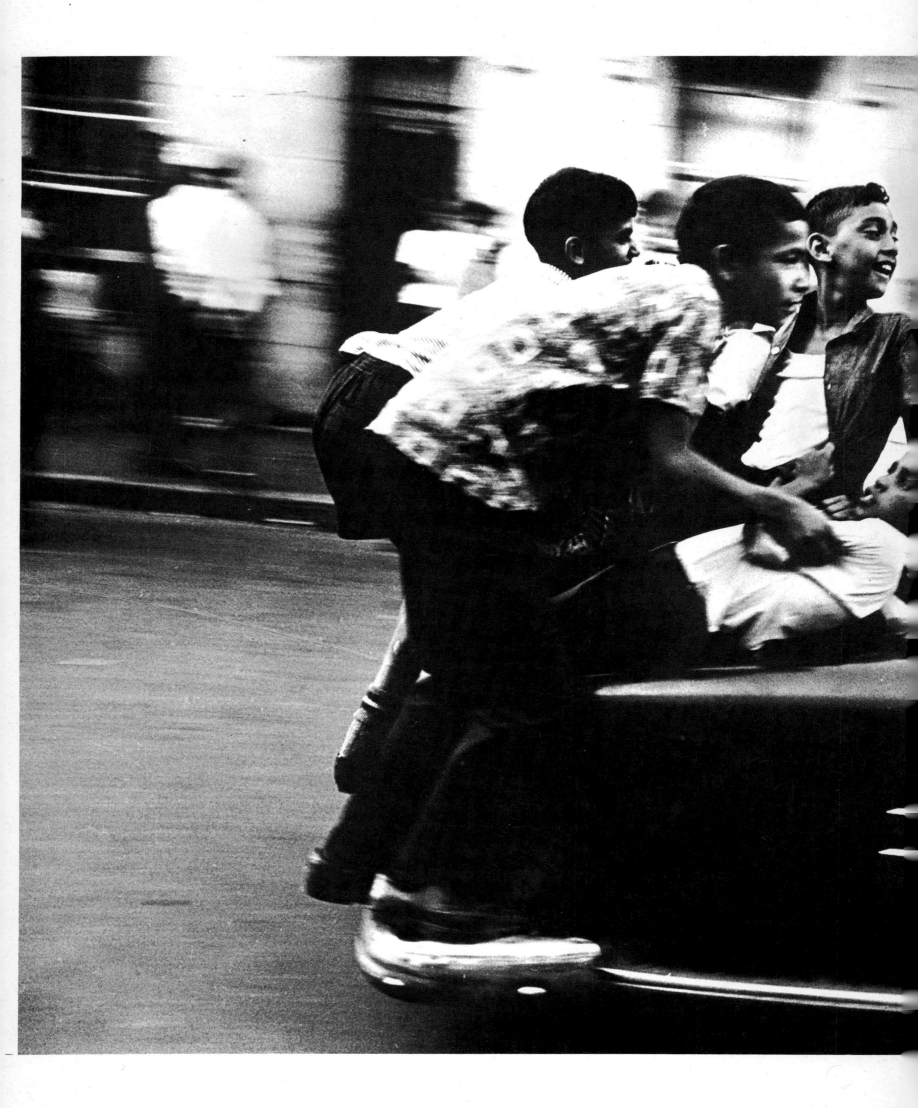

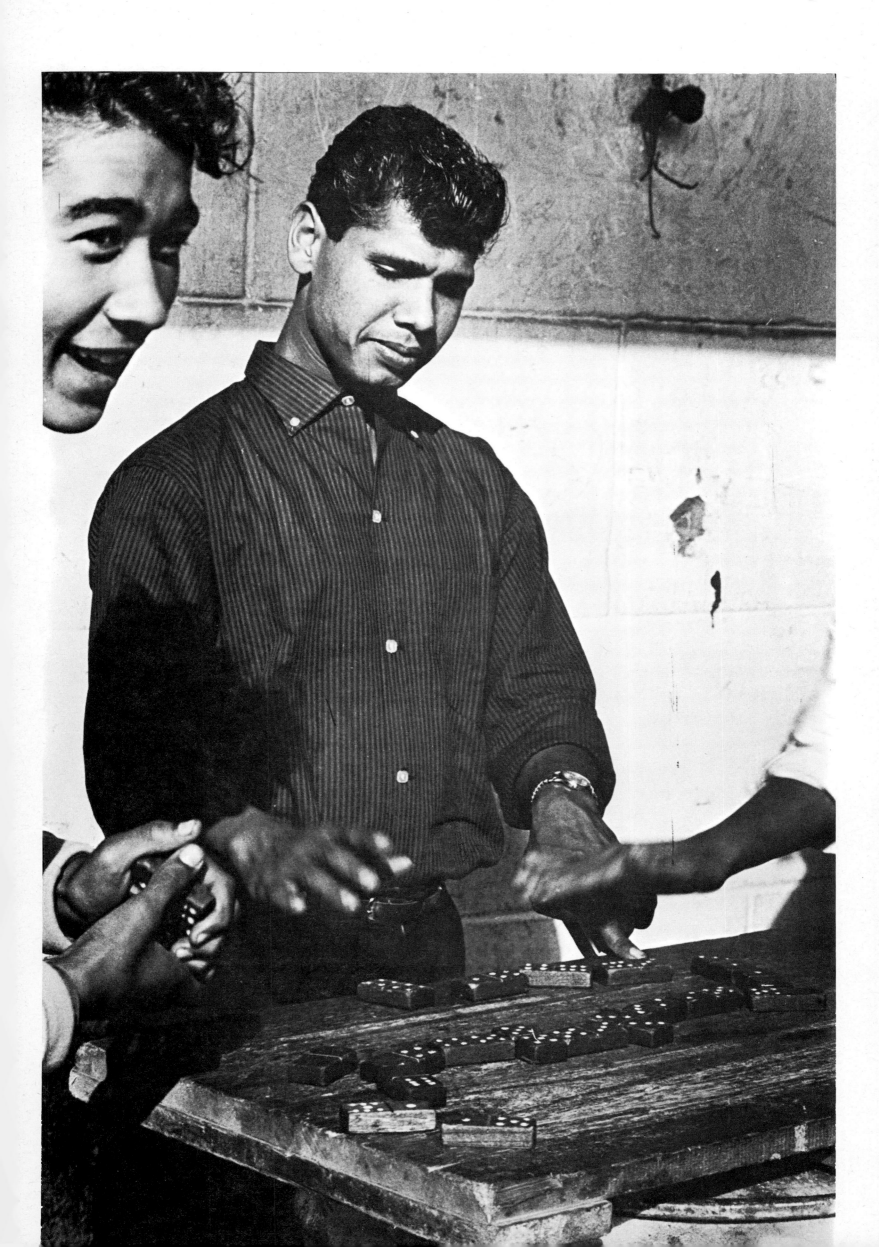

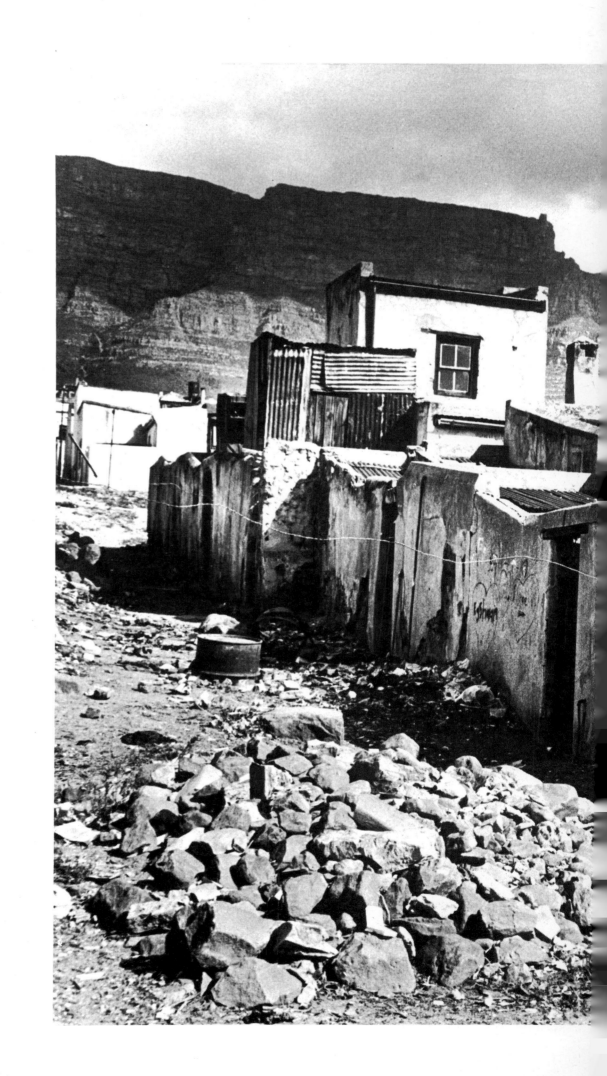

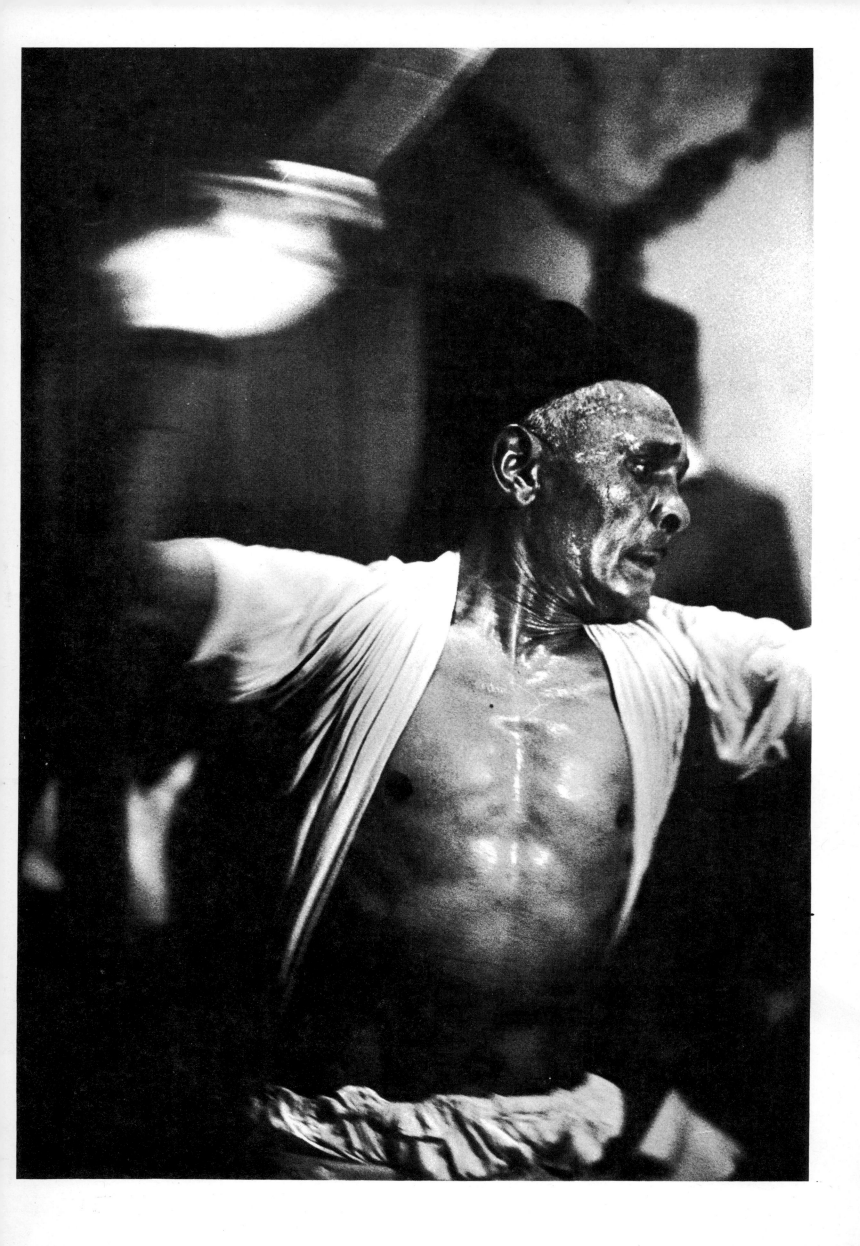

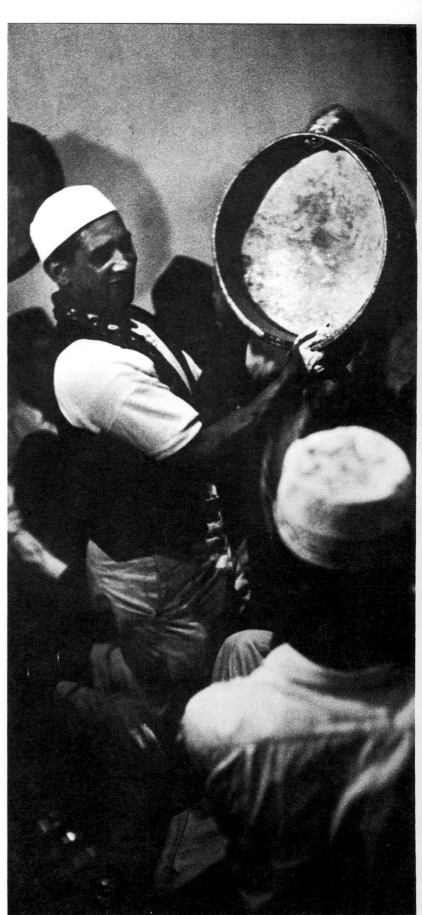

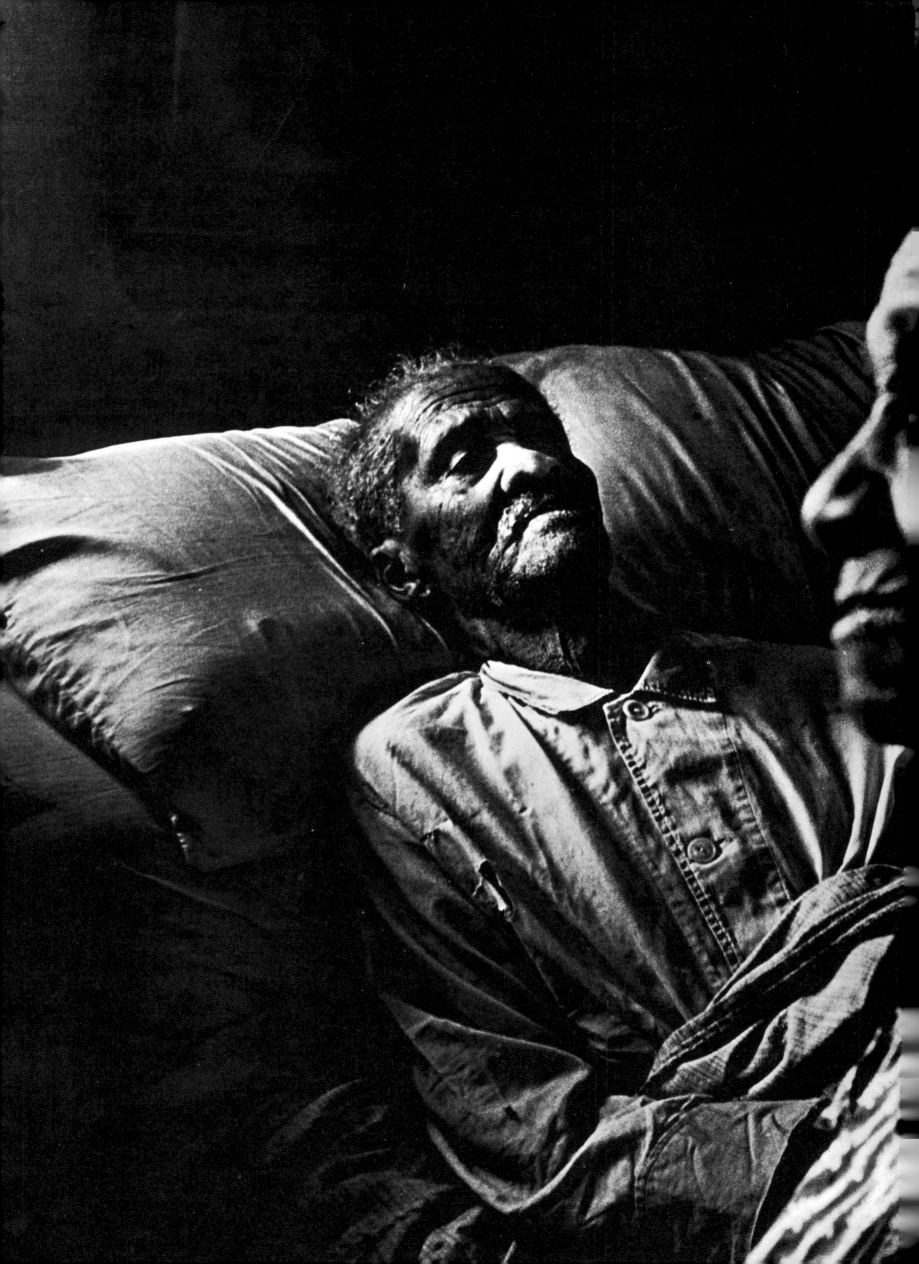